Love and Longing

A collection of classic poetry and prose

INTRODUCED BY

Jacqueline Wilson

EDITED BY

Kate Agnew

First published in the UK in 2004 by Wizard Books Ltd,
an imprint of Icon Books

This edition published in the USA in 2011
by Totem Books, an imprint of
Icon Books Ltd, Omnibus Business Centre,
39–41 North Road, London N7 9DP
email: info@iconbooks.co.uk
www.iconbooks.co.uk

Sold in the UK, Europe, South Africa and Asia
by Faber & Faber Ltd, Bloomsbury House,
74–77 Great Russell Street,
London WC1B 3DA or their agents

Distributed in the UK, Europe, South Africa and Asia
by TBS Ltd, TBS Distribution Centre, Colchester Road,
Frating Green, Colchester CO7 7DW

Published in Australia in 2004
by Allen & Unwin Pty Ltd,
PO Box 8500, 83 Alexander Street,
Crows Nest, NSW 2065

Distributed in the USA by
Consortium Book Sales & Distribution
The Keg House
34 Thirteenth Avenue NE, Suite 101
Minneapolis, Minnesota 55413-1007

Distributed in Canada by Penguin Books Canada,
90 Eglinton Avenue East, Suite 700,
Toronto, Ontario M4P 2Y3

ISBN: 978-1-84046-523-5

Introduction copyright © 2004 Jacqueline Wilson
This anthology copyright © 2004 Kate Agnew

Typeset by Wayzgoose

Printed and bound by CPI Mackays, Chatham ME5 8TD

Kate Agnew read English at the University of Oxford, has chaired the Children's Booksellers Association and has served as a judge for the Smarties Award and the Whitbread Prize. She was a contributor to the *Cambridge Guide to Children's Books* and co-wrote *Children at War* with Geoff Fox. In 1999 she won a special British Book Award for her contribution to the National Year of Reading.

Jacqueline Wilson has been on countless shortlists and won numerous awards, including the Smarties Prize, the Sheffield Children's Book Award and the Children's Book Award for *Double Act. The Illustrated Mum* was on the shortlist for the 1999 Whitbread Children's Book Award and won the 1999 Children's Book of the Year at the British Book Awards and the *Guardian* Children's Fiction Award. Four of her books were featured on the recent BBC 'Big Read' Top 100 poll. In June 2002 Jacqueline was given an OBE for services to literacy in schools.

Contents

Introduction

Love and Longing – that's what poetry is all about! I bet falling in love is the only time most of us are ever inspired to write poetry ourselves. I certainly wrote quite a few embarrassingly bad poems in my teens, though usually I had enough sense to keep them to myself. I'd write them down in my diary, not plucking up the courage to give them to the objects of my affections! I received a few love poems but I'm afraid my sweethearts weren't budding Shakespeares either. I was touched and flattered, but I couldn't help having a private giggle too. My name Jacqueline doesn't exactly lend itself to poetic expression. Oh Jacqueline, Will you be mine? is okay, if uninspired. Oh Jacqueline, you look so fine! isn't too great. Oh Jacqueline, Will you give me a good time? is pretty dire!

People want to write poems when they fall in love because it's such an exciting and wonderful feeling that you want to find some way of expressing it. The trouble is, all the great poets have got there before us! Maybe it makes more sense to read real poetry about love, rather than writing our own.

I've had a wonderful browse through this delightfully comprehensive anthology. The first poem I came across was an old favourite, Elizabeth Barrett Browning's Sonnet 43. I've always found Elizabeth and Robert Browning's real life story immensely romantic, and I'm an admirer of their poems. I once learnt Sonnet 43 by heart and actually mumbled it in the ear of a long-ago boyfriend. I can still recite it – but do you know something awful, I can't even remember the name of the boy I once thought I loved so much. That's another lesson to learn. True love doesn't always last. True love poetry lives on and on and on!

I think the most beautiful poem in this book is Alfred, Lord Tennyson's *Summer Night*. You can whisper it like an incantation – or an enticement! We have such a simplistic idea about the Victorians and their repressed attitudes when we only have to open their books to realise they knew a thing or two when it came to passion. The Brontë sisters, plain little parson's daughters, wrote passionate prose with a vengeance. There are extracts from plays too, including *Romeo and Juliet*, the most famous star-crossed teenage lovers in literature. There are many wonderful Shakespeare sonnets, most of which have to be worked at slowly, their full rich meaning needing to be patiently teased out. There are other short quirky poems that can be understood at a glance, like the heartfelt anonymous sixteenth-century poem:

> O western wind, when wilt thou blow
> That the small rain down can rain?
> Christ, that my love were in my arms
> And I in my bed again!

That's what's so interesting about this anthology, its sheer variety. There are beautiful ornate poems by several Lords, and even a Queen, and yet there are simple direct poems in everyday life language like *Sally in our Alley*. There's a charming poem by Anna Seward for her friend Honora, there's the sad and searing *Ballad of Reading Gaol* by Oscar Wilde, and there are two wonderfully contrasting poems about managing without your loved one by Charlotte Mew and Alice Meynell. There's even a love poem where the narrator insists over and over again I do not love Thee. I know one thing – I do love this anthology, and hope you will too.

Jacqueline Wilson, *October 2003*

How Do
I Love Thee?

Sonnet 43

How do I love thee? Let me count the ways.
I love thee to the depth and breadth and height
My soul can reach, when feeling out of sight
For the ends of being and ideal grace.
I love thee to the level of everyday's
Most quiet need, by sun and candlelight.
I love thee freely, as men strive for right;
I love thee purely, as they turn from praise.
I love thee with the passion put to use
In my old griefs, and with my childhood's faith.
I love thee with a love I seemed to lose
With my lost saints – I love thee with the breath,
Smiles, tears, of all my life! – and, if God choose,
I shall but love thee better after death.

Elizabeth Barrett Browning (1806–61)

The Good-Morrow

I wonder by my troth, what thou, and I
    Did, till we loved? Were we not weaned till then?
But sucked on country pleasures, childishly?
    Or snorted we in the seven sleepers' den?
'Twas so; but this, all pleasures fancies be.
If ever any beauty I did see,
Which I desired, and got, 'twas but a dream of thee.

And now good morrow to our waking souls,
    Which watch not one another out of fear;
For love all love of other sights controls,
    And makes one little room, an everywhere.
Let sea-discoverers to new worlds have gone,
Let maps to other, worlds on worlds have shown,
Let us possess one world; each hath one, and is one.

My face in thine eye, thine in mine appears,
    And true plain hearts do in the faces rest,
Where can we find two better hemispheres
    Without sharp north, without declining west?
Whatever dies, was not mixed equally;
If our two loves be one, or thou and I
Love so alike that none do slacken, none can die.

John Donne (1572–1631)

An Entire Devotion

Letter to Fanny Brawne, March 1820?

Sweetest Fanny,

You fear, sometimes, I do not love you so much as you wish? My dear Girl I love you ever and ever and without reserve. The more I have known you the more have I lov'd. In every way – even my jealousies have been agonies of Love, in the hottest fit I ever had I would have died for you. I have vex'd you too much. But for Love! Can I help it? You are always new. The last of your kisses was ever the sweetest; the last smile the brightest; the last movement the gracefullest. When you pass'd my window home yesterday, I was fill'd with as much admiration as if I had then seen you for the first time. You uttered a half complaint once that I only lov'd your Beauty. Have I nothing else then to love in you but that? Do not I see a heart naturally furnish'd with wings imprison itself with me? No ill prospect has been able to turn your thoughts a moment from me. This perhaps should be as much a subject of sorrow as joy – but I will not talk of that. Even if you did not love me I could not help an entire devotion to you: how much more deeply then must I feel for you knowing you love me. My Mind has been the most discontented and restless one that ever was put into a body too small for it. I never felt my Mind repose upon anything with complete and undistracted enjoyment – upon no person but you. When you are in the room my thoughts never fly out of window: you always concentrate my whole senses. The anxiety shown about our Love in your last note is an immense pleasure to me; however you must not suffer such speculations to molest you any more: not will I any more believe you can have the least pique against me. Brown is gone out – but here is Mrs Wylie – when she is gone I shall be awake for you. – Remembrances to your Mother.

Your affectionate
J. Keats

John Keats (1795–1821)

My True-Love Hath My Heart

My true-love hath my heart and I have his,
  By just exchange one for the other given:
I hold his dear, and mine he cannot miss;
  There never was a bargain better driven.
His heart in me keeps me and him in one;
  My heart in him his thoughts and senses guides:
He loves my heart, for once it was his own;
  I cherish his because in me it bides.
His heart his wound received from my sight;
  My heart was wounded with his wounded heart;
For as from me on him his hurt did light,
  So still, methought, in me his hurt did smart:
    Both equal hurt, in this change sought our bliss,
    My true love hath my heart and I have his.

Philip Sidney (1554–86)

Love is Enough

Love is enough: though the world be a-waning,
And the woods have no voice but the voice of complaining,
　　Though the sky be too dark for dim eyes to discover
The gold-cups and daisies fair blooming thereunder,
Though the hills be held shadows, and the sea a dark wonder,
　　And this day draw a veil over all deeds passed over,
Yet their hands shall not tremble, their feet shall not falter;
The void shall not weary, the fear shall not alter
　　These lips and these eyes of the loved and the lover.

William Morris (1834–96)

Love is and was my Lord and King

Love is and was my Lord and King,
    And in his presence I attend
    To hear the tidings of my friend,
Which every hour his couriers bring.

Love is and was my King and Lord,
    And will be, tho' as yet I keep
    Within his court on earth, and sleep
Encompassed by his faithful guard,

And hear at times a sentinel
    Who moves about from place to place,
    And whispers to the worlds of space,
In the deep night, that all is well.

In Memoriam
Alfred, Lord Tennyson (1809–92)

Set me as a seal upon thine heart

Set me as a seal upon thine heart, as a seal upon thine arm: For love is strong as death; Jealousy is cruel as the grave: The coals thereof are coals of fire, Which hath a most vehement flame.

Many waters cannot quench love, Neither can the floods drown it: If a man would give all the substance of his house for love, It would utterly be contemned.

The Bible, The Song of Solomon, Chapter 8: 6–7
The King James Version (1611)

Too Wise to Woo Peaceably

(LEONATO's *garden*)

BENEDICK

Sweet Beatrice, wouldst thou come when I called
thee?

BEATRICE

Yea, signior, and depart when you bid me.

BENEDICK

O, stay but till then!

BEATRICE

'Then' is spoken; fare you well now: and yet,
ere I go, let me go with that I came; which is,
with knowing what hath passed between you
and Claudio.

BENEDICK

Only foul words; and thereupon I will kiss thee.

BEATRICE

Foul words is but foul wind, and foul wind is but
foul breath, and foul breath is noisome; therefore
I will depart unkissed.

BENEDICK

Thou hast frighted the word out of his right sense,
so forcible is thy wit. But I must tell thee plainly,
Claudio undergoes my challenge; and either I must
shortly hear from him, or I will subscribe him a
coward. And, I pray thee now, tell me for which of
my bad parts didst thou first fall in love with me?

BEATRICE

> For them all together; which maintained so politic a state of evil that they will not admit any good part to intermingle with them. But for which of my good parts did you first suffer love for me?

BENEDICK

> Suffer love – a good epithet! I do suffer love indeed, for I love thee against my will.

BEATRICE

> In spite of your heart, I think; alas, poor heart! If you spite it for my sake, I will spite it for yours; for I will never love that which my friend hates.

BENEDICK

> Thou and I are too wise to woo peaceably.

Much Ado About Nothing, Act 5 Scene 2
William Shakespeare (1564–1616)

The Romantic Hero

And was Mr Rochester now ugly in my eyes? No, reader: gratitude, and many associations, all pleasurable and genial, made his face the object I best liked to see; his presence in a room was more cheering than the brightest fire. Yet I had not forgotten his faults; indeed, I could not, for he brought them frequently before me. He was proud, sardonic, harsh to inferiority of every description: in my secret soul I knew that his great kindness to me was balanced by unjust severity to many others. He was moody, too; unaccountably so; I more than once, when sent for to read to him, found him sitting in his library alone, with his head bent on his folded arms; and, when he looked up, a morose, almost a malignant, scowl blackened his features. But I believed that his moodiness, his harshness, and his former faults of morality (I say former?, for now he seemed corrected of them) had their source in some cruel cross of fate. I believed he was naturally a man of better tendencies, higher principles, and purer tastes than such as circumstances had developed, education instilled, or destiny encouraged. I thought there were excellent materials in him; though for the present they hung together somewhat spoiled and tangled. I cannot deny that I grieved for his grief, whatever that was, and would have given much to assuage it.

Jane Eyre
Charlotte Brontë (1816–55)

Miss Hale is Hurt

He could not sympathise with her. His anger had not abated; it was rather rising the more as his sense of immediate danger was passing away. The distant clank of the soldiers was heard just five minutes too late to make this vanished mob feel the power of authority and order. He hoped they would see the troops, and be quelled by the thought of their narrow escape. While these thoughts crossed his mind, Margaret clung to the doorpost to steady herself: but a film came over her eyes – he was only just in time to catch her. 'Mother – mother!' cried he; 'Come down – they are gone, and Miss Hale is hurt!' He bore her into the dining-room, and laid her on the sofa there; laid her down softly, and looking on her pure white face, the sense of what she was to him came upon him so keenly that he spoke it out in his pain:

'Oh, my Margaret – my Margaret! No one can tell what you are to me! Dead – cold as you lie there, you are the only woman I ever loved! Oh, Margaret – Margaret!'

Inarticulately as he spoke, kneeling by her, and rather moaning than saying the words, he started up, ashamed of himself, as his mother came in. She saw nothing, but her son a little paler, a little sterner than usual.

North and South
Elizabeth Gaskell (1810–65)

To Anthea, Who May Command
Him Anything

Bid me to live, and I will live
    Thy Protestant to be;
Or bid me love, and I will give
    A loving heart to thee.

A heart as soft, a heart as kind,
    A heart as sound and free
As in the whole world thou canst find,
    That heart I'll give to thee.

Bid that heart stay, and it will stay
    To honour thy decree:
Or bid it languish quite away,
    And 't shall do so for thee.

Bid me to weep, and I will weep
    While I have eyes to see:
And, having none, yet will I keep
    A heart to weep for thee.

Bid me despair, and I'll despair
    Under that cypress-tree:
Or bid me die, and I will dare
    E'en death to die for thee.

Thou art my life, my love my heart,
    The very eyes of me:
And hast command of every part
    To live and die for thee.

Robert Herrick (1591–1674)

To Sapho

Sapho, I will choose to go
Where the northern winds do blow
Endless ice, and endless snow;
Rather than I once would see
But a winter's face in thee, –
To benumb my hopes and me.

Robert Herrick (1591–1674)

To ——
One Word Is Too Often Profaned

One word is too often profaned
For me to profane it;
One feeling too falsely disdained
For thee to disdain it;
One hope is too like despair
For prudence to smother;
And pity from thee more dear
Than that from another.

I can give not what men call love;
But wilt thou accept not
The worship the heart lifts above
And the heavens reject not, –
The desire of the moth for the star,
Of the night for the morrow,
The devotion to something afar
From the sphere of our sorrow?

Percy Bysshe Shelley (1792–1822)

Romance

I will make you brooches and toys for your delight
Of bird-song at morning and star-shine at night.
I will make a palace fit for you and me,
Of green days in forests and blue days at sea.

I will make my kitchen, and you shall keep your room,
Where white flows the river and bright blows the broom,
And you shall wash your linen and keep your body white
In rainfall at morning and dewfall at night.

And this shall be for music when no one else is near,
The fine song for singing, the rare song to hear!
That only I remember, that only you admire,
Of the broad road that stretches and the roadside fire.

Robert Louis Stevenson (1850–94)

A Church Romance

She turned in the high pew, until her sight
Swept the west gallery, and caught its row
Of music-men with viol, book, and bow
Against the sinking sad tower-window light.

She turned again; and in her pride's despite
One strenuous viol's inspirer seemed to throw
A message from his string to her below,
Which said: 'I claim thee as my own forthright!'

Thus their hearts' bond began, in due time signed.
And long years thence, when Age had scared Romance,
At some old attitude of his or glance
That gallery-scene would break upon her mind,
With him as minstrel, ardent, young, and trim,
Bowing 'New Sabbath' or 'Mount Ephraim'.

                        Thomas Hardy (1840–1928)

23

The Love Unfeigned

O yonge, fresshe folkes, he or she,
In which that love up groweth with youre age,
Repeyreth[1] hom fro worldly vanyte,
And of youre herte up casteth the visage
To thilke God that after his ymage
Yow made, and thynketh al nys but a faire,
This world that passeth soone as floures faire.

And loveth him the which that right for love
Upon a crois, our soules for to beye,[2]
First starf,[3] and roos, and sit in hevene above;
For he nyl falsen no wight, dar I seye,
That wol his herte al holly on hym leye.
And syn he best to love is, and most meke,
What nedeth feyned loves for to seke?

Geoffrey Chaucer (*c.* 1343–1400)

---

[1] return
[2] redeem
[3] died

Lochinvar

O young Lochinvar is come out of the west,
Through all the wide border his steed was the best;
And save his good broad-sword he weapons had none,
He rode all unarmed, and he rode all alone.
So faithful in love, and so dauntless in war,
There never was knight like the young Lochinvar.

He stayed not for brake, and he stopped not for stone,
He swam the Eske river where ford there was none;
But ere he alighted at Netherby gate,
The bride had consented, the gallant came late:
For a laggard in love, and a dastard in war,
Was to wed the fair Ellen of brave Lochinvar.

So boldly he entered the Netherby Hall,
Among bride's-men, and kinsmen, and brothers and all:
Then spoke the bride's father, his hand on his sword,
(For the poor craven bridegroom said never a word,)
'O come ye in peace here, or come ye in war,
Or to dance at our bridal, young Lord Lochinvar?'

'I long wooed your daughter, my suit you denied; –
Love swells like the Solway, but ebbs like its tide –
And now I am come, with this lost love of mine,
To lead but one measure, drink one cup of wine.
There are maidens in Scotland more lovely by far,
That would gladly be bride to the young Lochinvar.'

The bride kissed the goblet: the knight took it up,
He quaffed off the wine, and he threw down the cup.
She looked down to blush, and she looked up to sigh,
With a smile on her lips and a tear in her eye.
He took her soft hand, ere her mother could bar, –
'Now tread we a measure!' said young Lochinvar.

So stately his form, and so lovely her face,
That never a hall such a galliard did grace;
While her mother did fret, and her father did fume
And the bridegroom stood dangling his bonnet and plume;
And the bride-maidens whispered, ''twere better by far
To have matched our fair cousin with young Lochinvar.'

One touch to her hand, and one word in her ear,
When they reached the hall-door, and the charger stood near;
So light to the croupe the fair lady he swung,
So light to the saddle before her he sprung!
'She is won! we are gone, over bank, bush, and scaur;
They'll have fleet steeds that follow,' quoth young Lochinvar.

There was mounting 'mong Graemes of the Netherby clan;
Forsters, Fenwicks, and Musgraves, they rode and they ran:
There was racing and chasing on Cannobie Lee,
But the lost bride of Netherby ne'er did they see.
So daring in love, and so dauntless in war,
Have ye e'er heard of gallant like young Lochinvar?

Marmion
Sir Walter Scott (1771–1832)

A Lover and His Lass

It was a lover and his lass
   With a hey and a ho and a hey nonino
That o'er the green corn-field did pass
   In springtime, the only pretty ring time
When birds do sing, Hey ding-a-ding ding
Sweet lovers love the spring

Between the acres of the rye
   With a hey and a ho and a hey nonino
These pretty country folks would lie
   In springtime, the only pretty ring time
When birds do sing, Hey ding-a-ding ding
Sweet lovers love the spring

This carol they began that hour
   With a hey and a ho and a hey nonino
How that a life was but a flower
   In springtime, the only pretty ring time
When birds do sing, Hey ding-a-ding ding
Sweet lovers love the spring

And therefore take the present time
   With a hey and a ho and a hey nonino
For love is crowned with the prime
   In springtime, the only pretty ring time
When birds do sing, Hey ding-a-ding ding
Sweet lovers love the spring.

As You Like It
William Shakespeare (1564–1616)

A Question

I asked if I got sick and died, would you
With my black funeral go walking too,
If you'd stand close to hear them talk or pray
When I'm let down into that steep bank of clay.

And, no, you said, for if you saw a crew
Of living idiots, pressing round that new
Oak coffin – they alive, I dead beneath
That board, – you'd rave and rend them with your teeth.

John Millington Synge (1871–1909)

An Evening Walk

He accompanied her up the hill, explaining to her the details of his forthcoming tenure of the other farm. They spoke very little of their mutual feeling; pretty phrases and warm expressions being probably unnecessary between such tried friends. Theirs was that substantial affection which arises (if any arises at all) when the two who are thrown together begin first by knowing the rougher sides of each other's character, and not the best till further on, the romance growing up in the interstices of a mass of hard prosaic reality. This good-fellowship – camaraderie – usually occurring through similarity of pursuits, is unfortunately seldom superadded to love between the sexes, because men and women associate, not in their labours, but in their pleasures merely. Where, however, happy circumstance permits its development, the compounded feeling proves itself to be the only love which is strong as death – that love which many waters cannot quench, nor the floods drown, beside which the passion usually called by the name is evanescent as steam.

Far From the Madding Crowd
Thomas Hardy (1840–1928)

Sonnet 116

Let me not to the marriage of true minds
Admit impediments. Love is not love
Which alters when it alteration finds,
Or bends with the remover to remove:
O no! it is an ever-fixèd mark
That looks on tempests and is never shaken;
It is the star to every wandering bark,
Whose worth's unknown, although his height be taken.
Love's not Time's fool, though rosy lips and cheeks
Within his bending sickle's compass come:
Love alters not with his brief hours and weeks,
But bears it out even to the edge of doom.
  If this be error and upon me proved,
  I never writ, nor no man ever loved.

William Shakespeare (1564–1616)

A Marriage Ring

The ring, so worn as you behold,
So thin, so pale, is yet of gold:
The passion such it was to prove –
Worn with life's care, love yet was love.

George Crabbe (1754–1832)

The Phoenix and the Turtle

Let the bird of loudest lay,
On the sole Arabian tree,
Herald sad and trumpet be,
To whose sound chaste wings obey.

But thou shrieking harbinger,
Foul precurrer of the fiend,
Augur of the fever's end,
To this troup come thou not near!

From this session interdict
Every fowl of tyrant wing,
Save the eagle, feathered king:
Keep the obsequy so strict.

Let the priest in surplice white,
That defunctive music can,
Be the death-divining swan,
Lest the requiem lack his right.

And thou treble-dated crow,
That thy sable gender makest
With the breath thou givest and takest,
'Mongst our mourners shalt thou go.

Here the anthem doth commence:
Love and constancy is dead;
Phoenix and the turtle fled
In a mutual flame from hence.

So they loved, as love in twain
Had the essence but in one;
Two distincts, division none:
Number there in love was slain.

Hearts remote, yet not asunder;
Distance, and no space was seen
'Twixt the turtle and his queen:
But in them it were a wonder.

So between them love did shine,
That the turtle saw his right
Flaming in the phoenix' sight;
Either was the other's mine.

Property was thus appalled,
That the self was not the same;
Single nature's double name
Neither two nor one was called.

Reason, in itself confounded,
Saw division grow together,
To themselves yet either neither,
Simple were so well compounded,

That it cried, 'how true a twain
Seemeth this concordant one!
Love hath reason, reason none,
If what parts can so remain.'

Whereupon it made this threne
To the phoenix and the dove,
Co-supremes and stars of love,
As chorus to their tragic scene.

THRENOS

Beauty, truth, and rarity,
Grace in all simplicity,
Here enclosed, in cinders lie.

Death is now the phoenix' nest
And the turtle's loyal breast
To eternity doth rest,

Leaving no posterity:
'Twas not their infirmity,
It was married chastity.

Truth may seem, but cannot be:
Beauty brag, but 'tis not she;
Truth and beauty buried be.

To this urn let those repair
That are either true or fair
For these dead birds sigh a prayer.

William Shakespeare (1564–1616)

I Do Not Love Thee

I do not love thee! – no! I do not love thee!
And yet when thou art absent I am sad;
    And envy even the bright blue sky above thee,
Whose quiet stars may see thee and be glad.

I do not love thee! – yet, I know not why,
Whate'er thou dost seems still well done, to me:
    And often in my solitude I sigh
That those I do love are not more like thee!

I do not love thee! – yet, when thou art gone,
I hate the sound (though those who speak be dear)
    Which breaks the lingering echo of the tone
Thy voice of music leaves upon my ear.

I do not love thee! – yet thy speaking eyes,
With their deep, bright, and most expressive blue,
    Between me and the midnight heaven arise,
Oftener than any eyes I ever knew.

I know I do not love thee! yet, alas!
Others will scarcely trust my candid heart;
    And oft I catch them smiling as they pass,
Because they see me gazing where thou art.

Caroline Elizabeth Sarah Norton (1808–76)

She Walks
in Beauty

Sonnet 18

Shall I compare thee to a summer's day?
Thou art more lovely and more temperate:
Rough winds do shake the darling buds of May,
And summer's lease hath all too short a date:
Sometime too hot the eye of heaven shines,
And often is his gold complexion dimmed;
And every fair from fair sometime declines,
By chance, or nature's changing course, untrimmed;
But thy eternal summer shall not fade,
Nor lose possession of that fair thou owest;
Nor shall Death brag thou wander'st in his shade,
When in eternal lines to time thou growest;
   So long as men can breathe, or eyes can see,
   So long lives this, and this gives life to thee.

William Shakespeare (1564–1616)

She Walks in Beauty

She walks in beauty, like the night
Of cloudless climes and starry skies;
And all that's best of dark and bright
Meet in her aspect and her eyes,
Thus mellowed to that tender light
Which heaven to gaudy day denies.

One shade the more, one ray the less,
Had half impaired the nameless grace
Which waves in every raven tress,
Or softly lightens o'er her face;
Where thoughts serenely sweet express
How pure, how dear their dwelling-place.

And on that cheek, and o'er that brow,
So soft, so calm, yet eloquent,
The smiles that win, the tints that glow,
But tell of days in goodness spent, –
A mind at peace with all below,
A heart whose love is innocent!

George Gordon, Lord Byron (1788–1824)

One Girl

Like the sweet apple which reddens upon
    the topmost bough,
Atop on the topmost twig, – which the
    pluckers forgot, somehow, –
Forgot it not, nay; but got it not, for none
    could get it till now.

Like the wild hyacinth flower which on the
    hills is found,
Which the passing feet of the shepherds
    forever tear and wound,
Until the purple blossom is trodden into the
    ground.

Sappho (7th century BC)
Translated by Dante Gabriel Rossetti (1828–82)

To Helen

Helen, thy beauty is to me
  Like those Nicean barks of yore,
That gently, o'er a perfumed sea,
  The weary, wayworn wanderer bore
  To his own native shore.

On desperate seas long wont to roam,
  Thy hyacinth hair, thy classic face,
Thy Naiad airs have brought me home
  To the glory that was Greece
  And the grandeur that was Rome.

Lo! in yon brilliant window-niche
  How statue-like I see thee stand,
The agate lamp within thy hand!
  Ah, Psyche, from the regions which
  Are Holy Land!

Edgar Allan Poe (1809–49)

A Song

Ask me no more where Jove bestows,
When June is past, the fading rose;
For in your beauty's orient deep
These flowers, as in their causes, sleep.

Ask me no more whither do stray
The golden atoms of the day;
For in pure love heaven did prepare
Those powders to enrich your hair.

Ask me no more whither doth haste
The nightingale, when May is past;
For in your sweet dividing throat
She winters, and keeps warm her note.

Ask me no more where those stars 'light,
That downwards fall in dead of night;
For in your eyes they sit, and there
Fixed become, as in their sphere.

Ask me no more if east or west
The phoenix builds her spicy nest;
For unto you at last she flies,
And in your fragrant bosom dies.

Thomas Carew (1594/5–1640)

Elegy

Written at the Sea-side, and Addressed to
Miss Honora Sneyd

I write, Honora, on the sparkling sand! –
The envious waves forbid the trace to stay:
Honora's name again adorns the strand!
Again the waters bear their prize away!

So Nature wrote her charms upon thy face,
The cheek's light bloom, the lip's envermeil'd dye,
And every gay, and every witching grace,
That Youth's warm hours, and Beauty's stores supply.

But Time's stern tide, with cold Oblivion's wave,
Shall soon dissolve each fair, each fading charm;
E'en Nature's self, so powerful, cannot save
Her own rich gifts from this o'erwhelming harm.

Love and the Muse can boast superior power,
Indelible the letters they shall frame;
They yield to no inevitable hour,
But will on lasting tablets write thy name.

Anna Seward (1747–1809)

Sally in Our Alley

Of all the girls that are so smart
   There's none like pretty Sally;
She is the darling of my heart,
   And she lives in our alley.
There is no lady in the land
   Is half so sweet as Sally;
She is the darling of my heart,
   And she lives in our alley.

Her father he makes cabbage-nets,
   And through the streets does cry 'em;
Her mother she sells laces long
   To such as please to buy 'em;
But sure such folks could ne'er beget
   So sweet a girl as Sally!
She is the darling of my heart,
   And she lives in our alley.

When she is by, I leave my work,
   I love her so sincerely;
My master comes like any Turk,
   And bangs me most severely:
But let him bang his bellyful,
   I'll bear it all for Sally;
She is the darling of my heart,
   And she lives in our alley.

Of all the days that's in the week
   I dearly love but one day –
And that's the day that comes betwixt
   A Saturday and Monday;

For then I'm drest all in my best
  To walk abroad with Sally;
She is the darling of my heart,
  And she lives in our alley.

My master carries me to church,
  And often am I blamèd
Because I leave him in the lurch
  As soon as text is namèd;
I leave the church in sermon-time
  And slink away to Sally;
She is the darling of my heart,
  And she lives in our alley.

When Christmas comes about again,
  O, then I shall have money;
I'll hoard it up, and box it all,
  I'll give it to my honey:
I would it were ten thousand pound,
  I'd give it all to Sally;
She is the darling of my heart,
  And she lives in our alley.

My master and the neighbours all
  Make game of me and Sally,
And, but for her, I'd better be
  A slave and row a galley;
But when my seven long years are out,
  O, then I'll marry Sally;
O, then we'll wed, and then we'll bed –
  But not in our alley!

Henry Carey (*c.*1690–1743)

Love Not Me For Comely Grace

Love not me for comely grace,
For my pleasing eye or face,
Nor for any outward part,
No, nor for a constant heart:
    For these may fail or turn to ill,
        So thou and I shall sever:

Keep, therefore, a true woman's eye,
And love me still but know not why –
    So hast thou the same reason still
        To dote upon me ever!

Anon. (17th century)

Sonnet 29

When in disgrace with fortune and men's eyes,
I all alone beweep my outcast state,
And trouble deaf Heaven with my bootless cries,
And look upon myself, and curse my fate,
Wishing me like to one more rich in hope,
Featured like him, like him with friends possessed,
Desiring this man's art, and that man's scope,
With what I most enjoy contented least:
Yet in these thoughts myself almost despising,
Haply I think on thee, – and then my state
(Like to the lark at break of day arising
From sullen earth) sings hymns at heaven's gate;
    For thy sweet love remembered such wealth brings
    That then I scorn to change my state with kings'.

William Shakespeare (1564–1616)

Fair is My Love and Cruel as She's Fair

Fair is my Love and cruel as she's fair;
Her brow-shades frown, although her eyes are sunny,
Her smiles are lightning, though her pride despair,
And her disdains are gall, her favours honey:
A modest maid, decked with a blush of honour,
Whose feet do tread green paths of youth and love;
The wonder of all eyes that look upon her,
Sacred on earth, designed a Saint above.
Chastity and Beauty, which were deadly foes,
Live reconcilèd friends within her brow;
And had she Pity to conjoin with those,
Then who had heard the plaints I utter now?
   For had she not been fair, and thus unkind,
    My Muse had slept, and none had known my mind.

Samuel Daniel (1562–1619)

Music, When Soft Voices Die

Music, when soft voices die,
Vibrates in the memory;
Odours, when sweet violets sicken,
Live within the sense they quicken.

Rose leaves, when the rose is dead,
Are heaped for the belovèd's bed;
And so thy thoughts, when thou art gone,
Love itself shall slumber on.

Percy Bysshe Shelley (1792–1822)

My Luve's Like a Red, Red Rose

O, my luve's like a red, red rose,
That's newly sprung in June;
O, my luve's like a melodie,
That's sweetly played in tune.

As fair art thou, my bonnie lass,
So deep in luve am I;
And I will luve thee still, my dear,
Till a' the seas gang dry.

Till a' the seas gang dry, my dear,
And the rocks melt wi' the sun!
And I will luve thee still, my dear,
While the sands o' life shall run.

And fare thee weel, my only luve!
And fare thee weel awhile!
And I will come again, my luve,
Tho' it were ten thousand mile!

Robert Burns (1759–96)

Time
of Roses

Time of Roses

It was not in the winter
    Our loving lot was cast;
It was the time of roses –
    We plucked them as we passed!

That churlish season never frowned
    On early lovers yet:
O no – the world was newly crowned
    With flowers when first we met!

'Twas twilight, and I bade you go,
    But still you held me fast;
It was the time of roses –
    We plucked them as we passed!

Thomas Hood (1798–1845)

It Was Deep April

It was deep April, and the morn
Shakespeare was born;
The world was on us, pressing sore;
My love and I took hands and swore,
Against the world, to be
Poets and lovers evermore,
To laugh and dream on Lethe's shore,
To sing to Charon in his boat,
Heartening the timid souls afloat;
Of judgement never to take heed,
But to those fast-locked souls to speed,
Who never from Apollo fled,
Who spent no hour among the dead;
Continually
With them to dwell,
Indifferent to heaven and hell.

Michael Field (Katherine Bradley (1846–1914)
and Edith Cooper (1862–1913))

At Castle Boterel

As I drive to the junction of lane and highway,
          And the drizzle bedrenches the waggonette,
I look behind at the fading byway,
          And see on its slope, now glistening wet,
                    Distinctly yet

Myself and a girlish form benighted
          In dry March weather. We climb the road
Beside a chaise. We had just alighted
          To ease the sturdy pony's load
                    When he sighed and slowed.

What we did as we climbed, and what we talked of
          Matters not much, nor to what it led, –
Something that life will not be balked of
          Without rude reason till hope is dead,
                    And feeling fled.

It filled but a minute. But was there ever
          A time of such quality, since or before,
In that hill's story? To one mind never,
          Though it has been climbed, foot-swift, foot-sore,
                    By thousands more.

Primaeval rocks form the road's steep border,
          And much have they faced there, first and last,
Of the transitory in Earth's long order;
          But what they record in colour and cast
                    Is – that we two passed.

And to me, though Time's unflinching rigour,
    In mindless rote, has ruled from sight
The substance now, one phantom figure
    Remains on the slope, as when that night
        Saw us alight.

I look and see it there, shrinking, shrinking,
    I look back at it amid the rain
For the very last time; for my sand is sinking,
    And I shall traverse old love's domain
        Never again.

Thomas Hardy (1840–1928)

It Rains

It rains, and nothing stirs within the fence
Anywhere through the orchard's untrodden, dense
Forest of parsley. The great diamonds
Of rain on the grassblades there is none to break,
Or the fallen petals further down to shake.

And I am nearly as happy as possible
To search the wilderness in vain though well,
To think of two walking, kissing there,
Drenched, yet forgetting the kisses of the rain:
Sad, too, to think that never, never again,

Unless alone, so happy shall I walk
In the rain. When I turn away, on its fine stalk
Twilight has fined to naught, the parsley flower
Figures, suspended still and ghostly white,
The past hovering as it revisits the light.

Edward Thomas (1878–1917)

Sea Love

Tide be runnin' the great world over:
    'Twas only last June month I mind that we
Was thinkin' the toss and the call in the breast of the lover
    So everlastin' as the sea.

Heer's the same little fishes that splutter and swim,
    Wi' the moon's old glim on the grey, wet sand:
An' him no more to me nor me to him
    Than the wind goin' over my hand.

Charlotte Mew (1869–1928)

The Hill

Breathless, we flung us on the windy hill,
    Laughed in the sun, and kissed the lovely grass.
    You said 'Through glory and ecstasy we pass;
Wind, sun, and earth remain, and birds sing still,
When we are old, are old ...' 'And when we die
    All's over that is ours; and life burns on
Through other lovers, other lips' said I,
    'Heart of my heart, our heaven is now, is won!'

'We are Earth's best, that learnt her lesson here.
    Life is our cry. We have kept the faith!' we said;
    'We shall go down with unreluctant tread
Rose-crowned into the darkness!' ... Proud we were,
And laughed, that had such brave true things to say.
    – And then you suddenly cried, and turned away.

Rupert Brooke (1887–1915)

When We Two Parted

When we two parted
    In silence and tears,
Half broken-hearted
    To sever for years,
Pale grew thy cheek and cold,
    Colder thy kiss;
Truly that hour foretold
    Sorrow to this.

The dew of the morning
    Sunk chill on my brow –
It felt like the warning
    Of what I feel now.
Thy vows are all broken,
    And light is thy fame:
I hear thy name spoken,
    And share in its shame.

They name thee before me,
    A knell to mine ear;
A shudder comes o'er me –
    Why wert thou so dear?
They know not I knew thee,
    Who knew thee too well:
Long, long shall I rue thee,
    Too deeply to tell.

In secret we met –
   In silence I grieve,
That thy heart could forget,
   Thy spirit deceive.
If I should meet thee
   After long years,
How should I greet thee?
   With silence and tears.

George Gordon, Lord Byron (1788–1824)

Love and Age

I played with you 'mid cowslips blowing,
    When I was six and you were four;
When garlands weaving, flower-balls throwing,
    Were pleasures soon to please no more.
Through groves and meads, o'er grass and heather,
    With little playmates, to and fro,
We wandered hand in hand together;
    But that was sixty years ago.

You grew a lovely roseate maiden,
    And still our early love was strong;
Still with no care our days were laden,
    They glided joyously along;
And I did love you very dearly,
    How dearly words want power to show;
I thought your heart was touched as nearly;
    But that was fifty years ago.

Then other lovers came around you,
    Your beauty grew from year to year,
And many a splendid circle found you
    The centre of its glimmering sphere.
I saw you then, first vows forsaking,
    On rank and wealth your hand bestow;
O, then I thought my heart was breaking! –
    But that was forty years ago.

And I lived on, to wed another:
    No cause she gave me to repine;
And when I heard you were a mother,
    I did not wish the children mine.

My own young flock, in fair progression,
    Made up a pleasant Christmas row:
My joy in them was past expression;
    But that was thirty years ago.

You grew a matron plump and comely,
    You dwelt in fashion's brightest blaze;
My earthly lot was far more homely;
    But I too had my festal days.
No merrier eyes have ever glistened
    Around the hearth-stone's wintry glow,
Than when my youngest child was christened;
    But that was twenty years ago.

Time passed. My eldest girl was married,
    And I am now a grandsire grey;
One pet of four years old I've carried
    Among the wild-flowered meads to play.
In our old fields of childish pleasure,
    Where now, as then, the cowslips blow,
She fills her basket's ample measure;
    And that is not ten years ago.

But though first love's impassioned blindness
    Has passed away in colder light,
I still have thought of you with kindness,
    And shall do, till our last good-night.
The ever-rolling silent hours
    Will bring a time we shall not know,
When our young days of gathering flowers
    Will be an hundred years ago.

Thomas Love Peacock (1785–1866)

A Quoi Bon Dire

Seventeen years ago you said
> Something that sounded like Good-bye:
> And everybody thinks you are dead
> > But I.

> So I as I grow stiff and cold
To this and that say Good-bye too;
> And everybody sees that I am old
> > But you.

> And one fine morning in a sunny lane
Some boy and girl will meet and kiss and swear
> That nobody can love their way again
> > While over there
You will have smiled, I shall have tossed your hair.

Charlotte Mew (1869–1928)

The Maid's Lament

I loved him not; and yet now he is gone,
      I feel I am alone.
I checked him while he spoke; yet, could he speak,
      Alas! I would not check.
For reasons not to love him once I sought,
      And wearied all my thought
To vex myself and him; I now would give
      My love, could he but live
Who lately lived for me, and when he found
      'Twas vain, in holy ground
He hid his face amid the shades of death.
      I waste for him my breath
Who wasted his for me; but mine returns,
      And this lorn bosom burns
With stifling heat, heaving it up in sleep,
      And waking me to weep
Tears that had melted his soft heart: for years
      Wept he as bitter tears.
'Merciful God!' such was his latest prayer,
      'These may she never share!'
Quieter is his breath, his breast more cold
      Than daisies in the mould,
Where children spell, athwart the churchyard gate,
      His name and life's brief date.
Pray for him, gentle souls, whoe'er you be,
      And, O, pray too for me!

Walter Savage Landor (1775–1864)

Renouncement

I must not think of thee; and, tired yet strong,
I shun the love that lurks in all delight –
    The love of thee – and in the blue heaven's height,
And in the dearest passage of a song.
Oh, just beyond the sweetest thoughts that throng
    This breast, the thought of thee waits hidden yet bright;
But it must never, never come in sight;
I must stop short of thee the whole day long.
But when sleep comes to close each difficult day,
    When night gives pause to the long watch I keep,
And all my bonds I needs must loose apart,
Must doff my will as raiment laid away, –
With the first dream that comes with the first sleep
    I run, I run, I am gathered to thy heart.

Alice Meynell (1847–1922)

Twice

I took my heart in my hand
    (O my love, O my love),
I said: Let me fall or stand,
    Let me live or die,
But this once hear me speak
    (O my love, O my love) –
Yet a woman's words are weak;
    You should speak, not I.

You took my heart in your hand
    With a friendly smile,
With a critical eye you scanned,
    Then set it down,
And said, 'It is still unripe,
    Better wait awhile;
Wait while the skylarks pipe,
    Till the corn grows brown.'

As you set it down it broke –
    Broke, but I did not wince;
I smiled at the speech you spoke,
    At your judgement I heard:
But I have not often smiled
    Since then, nor questioned since,
Nor cared for cornflowers wild,
    Nor sung with the singing bird.

I take my heart in my hand,
    O my God, O my God,
My broken heart in my hand:
    Thou hast seen, judge thou.
My hope was written on sand,
    O my God, O my God:
Now let thy judgement stand –
    Yea, judge me now.

This contemned of a man,
    This marred one heedless day,
This heart take thou to scan
    Both within and without:
Refine with fire its gold,
    Purge thou its dross away –
Yea, hold it in thy hold,
    Whence none can pluck it out.

I take my heart in my hand –
    I shall not die, but live –
Before thy face I stand;
    I, for thou callest such:
All that I have I bring,
    All that I am I give,
Smile thou and I shall sing,
    But shall not question much.

Christina Georgina Rossetti (1830–94)

Break, Break, Break

Break, break, break,
　　On thy cold grey stones, O sea!
And I would that my tongue could utter
　　The thoughts that arise in me.

O, well for the fisherman's boy,
　　That he shouts with his sister at play!
O, well for the sailor lad,
　　That he sings in his boat on the bay!

And the stately ships go on
　　To their haven under the hill;
But O for the touch of a vanished hand,
　　And the sound of a voice that is still!

Break, break, break,
　　At the foot of thy crags, O sea!
But the tender grace of a day that is dead
　　Will never come back to me.

Alfred, Lord Tennyson (1809–92)

Love and Life

All my past life is mine no more;
   The flying hours are gone,
Like transitory dreams given o'er,
Whose images are kept in store
   By memory alone.

The time that is to come is not;
   How can it then be mine?
The present moment's all my lot;
And that, as fast as it is got,
   Phillis, is only thine.

Then talk not of inconstancy,
   False hearts, and broken vows;
If I by miracle can be
This live-long minute true to thee,
   'Tis all that Heaven allows.

John Wilmot, Earl of Rochester (1647–80)

Come to Me
in Dreams,
My Love

O Western Wind, When Wilt Thou Blow

O western wind, when wilt thou blow
That the small rain down can rain?
Christ, that my love were in my arms
And I in my bed again!

Anon. (16th century)

Stanzas

Oh, come to me in dreams, my love!
  I will not ask a dearer bliss;
Come with the starry beams, my love,
  And press mine eyelids with thy kiss.

'Twas thus, as ancient fables tell,
  Love visited a Grecian maid,
Till she disturbed the sacred spell,
  And woke to find her hopes betrayed.

But gentle sleep shall veil my sight,
  And Psyche's lamp shall darkling be.
When, in the visions of the night,
  Thou dost renew thy vows to me.

Then come to me in dreams, my love,
  I will not ask a dearer bliss:
Come with the starry beams, my love,
  And press mine eyelids with thy kiss.

Mary Wollstonecraft Shelley (1797–1851)

Gallop apace, you fiery-footed steeds

(*A Room in* CAPULET's *House*)

[*Enter* JULIET]

JULIET

    Gallop apace, you fiery-footed steeds,
    Towards Phoebus' lodging; such a waggoner
    As Phaeton would whip you to the west
    And bring in cloudy night immediately. –
    Spread thy close curtain, love-performing night!
    That rude eyes may wink, and Romeo
    Leap to these arms, untalked of and unseen. –
    Lovers can see to do their amorous rites
    By their own beauties: or, if love be blind,
    It best agrees with night. – Come, civil night,
    Thou sober-suited matron, all in black,
    And learn me how to lose a winning match,
    Played for a pair of stainless maidenhoods:
    Hood my unmanned blood, bating in my cheeks,
    With thy black mantle; till strange love, grown bold,
    Think true love acted simple modesty.
    Come, night; – come, Romeo; – come, thou day in night;
    For thou wilt lie upon the wings of night
    Whiter than new snow on a raven's back. –
    Come, gentle night; – come, loving, black-browed night,
    Give me my Romeo; and, when he shall die,
    Take him and cut him out in little stars,
    And he will make the face of heaven so fine
    That all the world will be in love with night,

And pay no worship to the garish sun. –
O, I have bought the mansion of a love,
But not possessed it; and, though I am sold,
Not yet enjoyed: so tedious is this day
As is the night before some festival
To an impatient child that hath new robes,
And may not wear them.

Romeo and Juliet, Act 3 Scene 2
William Shakespeare (1564–1616)

Bridal Song

O come, soft rest of cares! come, Night!
  Come, naked Virtue's only tire,
The reapèd harvest of the light
  Bound up in sheaves of sacred fire.
    Love calls to war:
      Sighs his alarms,
    Lips his swords are,
      The field his arms.

Come, Night, and lay thy velvet hand
  On glorious Day's outfacing face;
And all thy crownèd flames command
  For torches to our nuptial grace.
    Love calls to war:
      Sighs his alarms,
    Lips his swords are,
      The field his arms.

George Chapman (1560–1634)

... And On My Eyes Dark Sleep By Night

Come, dark-eyed Sleep, thou child of Night,
Give me thy dreams, thy lies;
Lead through the horny portal white
The pleasure day denies.

O bring the kiss I could not take
From lips that would not give;
Bring me the heart I could not break,
The bliss for which I live.

I care not if I slumber blest
By fond delusion; nay,
Put me on Phaon's lips to rest,
And cheat the cruel day!

Michael Field (Katherine Bradley (1846–1914)
and Edith Cooper (1862–1913))

False Though She Be

False though she be to me and love,
    I'll ne'er pursue revenge;
For still the charmer I approve,
    Though I deplore her change.

In hours of bliss we oft have met:
    They could not always last;
And though the present I regret,
    I'm grateful for the past.

William Congreve (1670–1729)

There is a Lady Sweet and Kind

There is a Lady sweet and kind,
Was never face so pleased my mind;
I did but see her passing by,
And yet I love her till I die.

Her gesture, motion, and her smiles,
Her wit, her voice my heart beguiles,
Beguiles my heart, I know not why,
And yet I love her till I die.

Cupid is wingèd and doth range,
Her country so my love doth change:
But change she earth, or change she sky,
Yet will I love her till I die.

Anon. (1607)

To Althea, from Prison

When Love with unconfinèd wings
   Hovers within my gates;
And my divine Althea brings
   To whisper at the grates;
When I lie tangled in her hair
   And fettered to her eye;
The birds that wanton in the air,
   Know no such liberty.

When flowing cups run swiftly round
   With no allaying Thames,
Our careless heads with roses bound,
   Our hearts with loyal flames;
When thirsty grief in wine we steep,
   When healths and draughts go free,
Fishes that tipple in the deep,
   Know no such liberty.

When (like committed linnets) I
   With shriller throat shall sing
The sweetness, mercy, Majesty,
   And glories of my king;
When I shall voice aloud, how good
   He is, how great should be;
Enlargèd winds that curl the Flood,
   Know no such liberty.

Stone walls do not a prison make,
  Nor iron bars a cage;
Minds innocent and quiet take
  That for an hermitage;
If I have freedom in my love,
  And in my soul am free;
Angels alone that soar above,
  Enjoy such liberty.

Richard Lovelace (1618–57/8)

I So Liked Spring

I so liked Spring last year
  Because you were here; –
   The thrushes too –
Because it was these you so liked to hear –
   I so liked you.

  This year's a different thing, –
   I'll not think of you.
But I'll like the Spring because it is simply Spring
   As the thrushes do.

        Charlotte Mew (1869–1928)

On Monsieur's Departure

I grieve and dare not show my discontent,
   I love and yet am forced to seem to hate,
I do, yet dare not say I ever meant,
   I seem stark mute but inwardly do prate.
I am and not, I freeze and yet am burned,
Since from myself another self I turned.

My care is like my shadow in the sun,
   Follows me flying, flies when I pursue it,
Stands and lies by me, doth what I have done.
   His too familiar care doth make me rue it.
No means I find to rid him from my breast,
Till by the end of things it be supprest.

Some gentler passion slide into my mind,
   For I am soft and made of melting snow;
Or be more cruel, love, and so be kind.
   Let me or float or sink, be high or low.
Or let me live with some more sweet content,
Or die and so forget what love ever meant.

Elizabeth I (1533–1603)

Lucy ii:
She Dwelt Among the Untrodden Ways

She dwelt among the untrodden ways
  Beside the springs of Dove,
A maid whom there were none to praise
  And very few to love:

A violet by a mossy stone
  Half hidden from the eye!
– Fair as a star, when only one
  Is shining in the sky.

She lived unknown, and few could know
  When Lucy ceased to be;
But she is in her grave, and, oh,
  The difference to me!

William Wordsworth (1770–1850)

Jenny Kissed Me

Jenny kissed me when we met,
  Jumping from the chair she sat in;
Time, you thief, who love to get
  Sweets into your list, put that in!
Say I'm weary, say I'm sad,
  Say that health and wealth have missed me,
Say I'm growing old, but add,
  Jenny kissed me.

Leigh Hunt (1784–1859)

Methought I Saw My Late Espousèd Saint

Methought I saw my late espousèd saint
    Brought to me like Alcestis from the grave,
    Whom Jove's great son to her glad husband gave,
    Rescued from death by force, though pale and faint.
Mine, as whom washed from spot of childbed taint
    Purification in the old law did save,
    And such as yet once more I trust to have
    Full sight of her in heaven without restraint,
Came vested all in white, pure as her mind.
    Her face was veiled, yet to my fancied sight
    Love, sweetness, goodness in her person shined
So clear as in no face with more delight.
    But O as to embrace me she inclined,
    I waked, she fled, and day brought back my night.

John Milton (1608–74)

The Apparition

My dead Love came to me, and said:
    'God gives me one hour's rest
To spend upon the earth with thee:
    How shall we spend it best?'

'Why, as of old,' I said, and so
    We quarrelled as of old.
But when I turned to make my peace
    That one short hour was told.

Stephen Phillips (1864–1915)

The Going

Why did you give no hint that night
That quickly after the morrow's dawn,
And calmly, as if indifferent quite,
You would close your term here, up and be gone
     Where I could not follow
     With wing of swallow
To gain one glimpse of you ever anon!

     Never to bid good-bye
     Or lip me the softest call,
Or utter a wish for a word, while I
Saw morning harden upon the wall,
     Unmoved, unknowing
     That your great going
Had place that moment, and altered all.

Why do you make me leave the house
And think for a breath it is you I see
At the end of the alley of bending boughs
Where so often at dusk you used to be;
     Till in darkening dankness
     The yawning blankness
Of the perspective sickens me!

     You were she who abode
     By those red-veined rocks far West,
You were the swan-necked one who rode
Along the beetling Beeny Crest,

And, reining nigh me,
Would muse and eye me,
While Life unrolled us its very best.

Why, then, latterly did we not speak,
Did we not think of those days long dead,
And ere your vanishing strive to seek
That time's renewal? We might have said,
'In this bright spring weather
We'll visit together
Those places that once we visited.'

Well, well! All's past amend,
Unchangeable. It must go.
I seem but a dead man held on end
To sink down soon ... O you could not know
That such swift fleeing
No soul foreseeing –
Not even I – would undo me so!

Thomas Hardy (1840–1928)

The Voice

Woman much missed, how you call to me, call to me,
Saying that now you are not as you were
When you had changed from the one who was all to me,
But as at first, when our day was fair.

Can it be you that I hear? Let me view you, then,
Standing as when I drew near to the town
Where you would wait for me: yes, as I knew you then,
Even to the original air-blue gown!

Or is it only the breeze, in its listlessness
Travelling across the wet mead to me here,
You being ever dissolved to wan wistlessness,
Heard no more again far or near?

  Thus I; faltering forward,
  Leaves around me falling,
Wind oozing thin through the thorn from norward,
  And the woman calling.

Thomas Hardy (1840–1928)

The Lost Mistress

All's over, then: does truth sound bitter
    As one at first believes?
Hark, 'tis the sparrows' good-night twitter
    About your cottage eaves!

And the leaf-buds on the vine are woolly,
    I noticed that, to-day;
One day more bursts them open fully
    – You know the red turns gray.

To-morrow we meet the same then, dearest?
    May I take your hand in mine?
Mere friends are we, – well, friends the merest
    Keep much that I resign:

For each glance of the eye so bright and black,
    Though I keep with heart's endeavour, –
Your voice, when you wish the snowdrops back,
    Though it stay in my soul for ever! –

Yet I will but say what mere friends say,
    Or only a thought stronger;
I will hold your hand but as long as all may,
    Or so very little longer!

Robert Browning (1812–89)

We'll Go No More A-Roving

So, we'll go no more a-roving
    So late into the night,
Though the heart be still as loving,
    And the moon be still as bright.

For the sword outwears its sheath,
    And the soul wears out the breast,
And the heart must pause to breathe,
    And love itself have rest.

Though the night was made for loving,
    And the day returns too soon,
Yet we'll go no more a-roving
    By the light of the moon.

George Gordon, Lord Byron (1788–1824)

The Enchantment

I did but look and love awhile,
    'Twas but for one half-hour;
Then to resist I had no will,
    And now I have no power.

To sigh and wish is all my ease;
    Sighs which do heat impart
Enough to melt the coldest ice,
    Yet cannot warm your heart.

O would your pity give my heart
    One corner of your breast,
'Twould learn of yours the winning art,
    And quickly steal the rest.

Thomas Otway (1652–85)

Give All
to Love

Summer Night

Now sleeps the crimson petal, now the white;
Nor waves the cypress in the palace walk;
Nor winks the gold fin in the porphyry font:
The firefly wakens: waken thou with me.

Now droops the milk-white peacock like a ghost,
And like a ghost she glimmers on to me.

Now lies the Earth all Danaë to the stars,
And all thy heart lies open unto me.

Now slides the silent meteor on, and leaves
A shining furrow, as thy thoughts in me.

Now folds the lily all her sweetness up,
And slips into the bosom of the lake:
So fold thyself, my dearest, thou, and slip
Into my bosom and be lost in me.

Alfred, Lord Tennyson (1809–92)

Palm Sonnet

ROMEO

> If I profane with my unworthiest hand
> This holy shrine, the gentle sin is this:
> My lips, two blushing pilgrims, ready stand
> To smooth that rough touch with a tender kiss.

JULIET

> Good pilgrim, you do wrong your hand too much,
> Which mannerly devotion shows in this;
> For saints have hands that pilgrims' hands do touch,
> And palm to palm is holy palmers' kiss.

ROMEO

> Have not saints lips, and holy palmers too?

JULIET

> Ay, pilgrim, lips that they must use in prayer.

ROMEO

> O then, dear saint, let lips do what hands do:
> They pray; grant thou, lest faith turn to despair.

JULIET

> Saints do not move, though grant for prayer's sake.

ROMEO

> Then move not, while my prayer's effect I take.

> [*They kiss*]

Romeo and Juliet, Act 1 Scene 5
William Shakespeare (1564–1616)

To Celia

Drink to me only with thine eyes,
    And I will pledge with mine;
Or leave a kiss but in the cup,
    And I'll not look for wine.
The thirst that from the soul doth rise
    Doth ask a drink divine:
But might I of Jove's nectar sup,
    I would not change for thine.

I sent thee late a rosy wreath,
    Not so much honouring thee,
As giving it a hope that there
    It could not withered be.
But thou thereon didst only breathe,
    And sent'st it back to me;
Since when it grows, and smells, I swear,
    Not of itself, but thee.

Ben Jonson (1572/3–1637)

Give All to Love

Give all to love;
Obey thy heart;
Friends, kindred, days,
Estate, good fame,
Plans, credit, and the Muse –
Nothing refuse.

'Tis a brave master;
Let it have scope:
Follow it utterly,
Hope beyond hope:
High and more high
It dives into noon,
With wing unspent,
Untold intent;
But it is a god,
Knows its own path,
And the outlets of the sky.

It was never for the mean;
It requireth courage stout,
Souls above doubt,
Valour unbending:
Such 'twill reward; –
They shall return
More than they were,
And ever ascending.

Leave all for love;
Yet, hear me, yet,
One word more thy heart behoved,
One pulse more of firm endeavour –
Keep thee to-day,
To-morrow, for ever,
Free as an Arab
Of thy beloved.

Cling with life to the maid;
But when the surprise,
First vague shadow of surmise,
Flits across her bosom young,
Of a joy apart from thee,
Free be she, fancy-free;
Nor thou detain her vesture's hem,
Nor the palest rose she flung
From her summer diadem.

Though thou loved her as thyself,
As a self of purer clay;
Though her parting dims the day,
Stealing grace from all alive;
Heartily know,
When half-gods go
The gods arrive.

Ralph Waldo Emerson (1803–82)

Maud

Come into the garden, Maud,
    For the black bat, Night, has flown,
Come into the garden, Maud,
    I am here at the gate alone;
And the woodbine spices are wafted abroad,
    And the musk of the roses blown.

For a breeze of morning moves,
    And the planet of Love is on high,
Beginning to faint in the light that she loves
    On a bed of daffodil sky,
To faint in the light of the sun she loves,
    To faint in his light, and to die.

All night have the roses heard
    The flute, violin, bassoon;
All night has the casement jessamine stirred
    To the dancers dancing in tune;
Till a silence fell with the waking bird,
    And a hush with the setting moon.

I said to the lily, 'There is but one
    With whom she has heart to be gay.
When will the dancers leave her alone?
    She is weary of dance and play.'
Now half to the setting moon are gone,
And half to the rising day;
    Low on the sand and loud on the stone
The last wheel echoes away.

I said to the rose, 'The brief night goes
   In babble and revel and wine.
O young lord-lover, what sighs are those
   For one that will never be thine?
But mine, but mine,' so I sware to the rose,
   'For ever and ever, mine.'

And the soul of the rose went into my blood,
   As the music clashed in the hall;
And long by the garden lake I stood,
   For I heard your rivulet fall
From the lake to the meadow and on to the wood,
   Our wood, that is dearer than all;

From the meadow your walks have left so sweet
   That whenever a March-wind sighs
He sets the jewel-print of your feet
   In violets blue as your eyes,
To the woody hollows in which we meet
   And the valleys of Paradise.

The slender acacia would not shake
   One long milk-bloom on the tree;
The white lake-blossom fell into the lake,
   As the pimpernel dozed on the lea;
But the rose was awake all night for your sake,
   Knowing your promise to me;
The lilies and roses were all awake,
   They sighed for the dawn and thee.

Queen rose of the rosebud garden of girls,
   Come hither, the dances are done,

In gloss of satin and glimmer of pearls,
    Queen lily and rose in one;
Shine out, little head, sunning over with curls.
    To the flowers, and be their sun.

There has fallen a splendid tear
    From the passion-flower at the gate.
She is coming, my dove, my dear;
    She is coming, my life, my fate;
The red rose cries, 'She is near, she is near;'
    And the white rose weeps, 'She is late;'
The larkspur listens, 'I hear, I hear;'
    And the lily whispers, 'I wait.'

She is coming, my own, my sweet;
    Were it ever so airy a tread,
My heart would hear her and beat,
    Were it earth in an earthy bed;
My dust would hear her and beat,
    Had I lain for a century dead;
Would start and tremble under her feet,
    And blossom in purple and red.

Alfred, Lord Tennyson (1809–92)

The Passionate Shepherd to His Love

Come live with me and be my love,
And we will all the pleasures prove
That hills and valleys, dale and field,
And all the craggy mountains yield.

There we will sit upon the rocks,
And see the shepherds feed their flocks,
By shallow rivers, to whose falls
Melodious birds sing madrigals.

Therewill I make thee beds of roses
And a thousand fragrant posies,
A cap of flowers, and a kirtle
Embroidered all with leaves of myrtle;

A gown made of the finest wool
Which from our pretty lambs we pull;
Fair lined slippers for the cold,
With buckles of the purest gold;

A belt of straw and ivy buds,
With coral clasps and amber studs;
And if these pleasures may thee move,
Come live with me, and be my love.

The shepherd swains shall dance and sing
For thy delight each May morning:
If these delights thy mind may move,
Then live with me and be my love.

Christopher Marlowe (1564–93)

My Sweetest Lesbia

My sweetest Lesbia, let us live and love,
And though the sager sort our deeds reprove,
Let us not weigh them. Heaven's great lamps do dive
Into their west, and straight again revive.
But, soon as once set is our little light,
Then must we sleep one ever-during night.

If all would lead their lives in love like me,
Then bloody swords and armour should not be;
No drum or trumpet peaceful sleeps should move,
Unless alarm came from the camp of Love:
But fools do live and waste their little light,
And seek with pain their ever-during night.

When timely death my life and fortune ends,
Let not my hearse be vext with mourning friends,
But let all lovers rich in triumph come
And with sweet pastimes grace my happy tomb:
And, Lesbia, close up thou my little light,
And crown with love my ever-during night.

Catullus (87–57 BC)
Translated by Thomas Campion (1567–1620)

The Reconcilement

Come, let us now resolve at last
    To live and love in quiet;
We'll tie the knot so very fast
    That Time shall ne'er untie it.

The truest joys they seldom prove
    Who free from quarrels live:
'Tis the most tender part of love
    Each other to forgive.

When least I seemed concerned, I took
    No pleasure nor no rest;
And when I feigned an angry look,
    Alas! I loved you best.

Own but the same to me – you'll find
    How blest will be our fate.
O to be happy – to be kind –
    Sure never is too late!

John Sheffield, Duke of Buckinghamshire (1649–1720)

Feste's Song

O mistress mine, where are you roaming?
O, stay and hear; your true love's coming,
    That can sing both high and low,
Trip no further, pretty sweeting,
Journeys end in lovers meeting,
    Every wise man's son doth know.

What is love? 'Tis not hereafter,
Present mirth hath present laughter,
    What's to come is still unsure,
In delay there lies not plenty,
Then, come kiss me, sweet and twenty,
    Youth's a stuff will not endure.

Twelfth Night
William Shakespeare (1564–1616)

Love Nowadayes

But nowadayes men can nat love sevennyght but they muste have all their desyres. That love may nat endure by reson, for where they bethe sone accorded and hasty, heete sone keelyth.[1] And ryght so faryth the love nowadayes, sone hote sone colde. Thys ys no stabylyté. But the olde love was nat so. For men and women coude love togydirs seven yerys, and no lycoures lustis was betwyxte them, and than was love trouthe and faythefulnes. And so in lyke wyse was used such love in kynge Arthurs dayes.

Wherefore I lykken love nowadayes unto sommer and wynter: for, lyke as the tone[2] ys colde and the othir ys hote, so faryth love nowadayes.

Le Morte D'Arthur
The Book of Sir Launcelot and Queen Guinevere
Sir Thomas Malory (d. 1471)

---

[1] cools   [2] the one

To His Coy Mistress

Had we but world enough, and time,
This coyness, lady, were no crime.
We would sit down and think which way
To walk, and pass our long love's day;
Thou by the Indian Ganges' side
Shouldst rubies find; I by the tide
Of Humber would complain. I would
Love you ten years before the Flood;
And you should, if you please, refuse
Till the conversion of the Jews.
My vegetable love should grow
Vaster than empires, and more slow.
An hundred years should go to praise
Thine eyes, and on thy forehead gaze;
Two hundred to adore each breast,
But thirty thousand to the rest;
An age at least to every part,
And the last age should show your heart.
For, lady, you deserve this state,
Nor would I love at lower rate.

But at my back I always hear
Time's winged chariot hurrying near;
And yonder all before us lie
Deserts of vast eternity.
Thy beauty shall no more be found,
Nor, in thy marble vault, shall sound
My echoing song; then worms shall try

That long preserved virginity,
And your quaint honour turn to dust,
And into ashes all my lust.
The grave's a fine and private place,
But none I think do there embrace.
Now therefore, while the youthful hue
Sits on thy skin like morning dew,
And while thy willing soul transpires
At every pore with instant fires,
Now let us sport us while we may;
And now, like am'rous birds of prey,
Rather at once our time devour,
Than languish in his slow-chapped power.
Let us roll all our strength, and all
Our sweetness, up into one ball;
And tear our pleasures with rough strife
Thorough the iron gates of life.
Thus, though we cannot make our sun
Stand still, yet we will make him run.

Andrew Marvell (1621–78)

The Flea

Mark but this flea, and mark in this,
How little that which thou deniest me is;
Me it sucked first, and now sucks thee,
And in this flea our two bloods mingled be.
Confess it, this cannot be said
A sin, or shame, or loss of maidenhead;
    Yet this enjoys before it woo,
    And pampered swells with one blood made of two;
    And this, alas! is more than we would do.

O stay, three lives in one flea spare,
Where we almost, yea, more than married are.
This flea is you and I, and this
Our marriage bed, and marriage temple is.
Though parents grudge, and you, we are met,
And cloistered in these living walls of jet.
    Though use make you apt to kill me,
    Let not to this self-murder added be,
    And sacrilege, three sins in killing three.

Cruel and sudden, hast thou since
Purpled thy nail in blood of innocence?
Wherein could this flea guilty be,
Except in that drop which it sucked from thee?
Yet thou triumph'st, and say'st that thou
Find'st not thyself nor me the weaker now.
    'Tis true; then learn how false fears be;
    Just so much honour, when thou yield'st to me,
    Will waste, as this flea's death took life from thee.

John Donne (1572–1631)

To His Coy Love

I pray thee, leave, love me no more,
　　Call home the heart you gave me!
I but in vain that saint adore
　　That can but will not save me.
These poor half-kisses kill me quite –
　　Was ever man thus servèd?
Amidst an ocean of delight
　　For pleasure to be starvèd?

Show me no more those snowy breasts
　　With azure riverets branchèd,
Where, whilst mine eye with plenty feasts,
　　Yet is my thirst not stanchèd;
O Tantalus, thy pains ne'er tell!
　　By me thou art prevented:
'Tis nothing to be plagued in Hell,
　　But thus in Heaven tormented.

Clip me no more in those dear arms,
　　Nor thy life's comfort call me,
O these are but too powerful charms,
　　And do but more enthral me!
But see how patient I am grown
　　In all this coil about thee:
Come, nice thing, let my heart alone,
　　I cannot live without thee!

Michael Drayton (1563–1631)

To a Lady Asking Him How Long He Would Love Her

It is not, Celia, in our power
  To say how long our love will last;
It may be we within this hour
  May lose those joys we now do taste;
The Blessèd, that immortal be,
From change in love are only free.

Then since we mortal lovers are,
  Ask not how long our love will last;
But while it does, let us take care
  Each minute be with pleasure past:
Were it not madness to deny
To live because we're sure to die?

Sir George Etherege (1635–91)

To One Persuading a Lady
to Marriage

Forbear, bold youth; all's heaven here,
  And what you do aver
To others courtship may appear,
  'Tis sacrilege to her.
She is a public deity;
  And were 't not very odd
She should dispose herself to be
  A petty household god?

First make the sun in private shine
  And bid the world adieu,
That so he may his beams confine
  In compliment to you:
But if of that you do despair,
  Think how you did amiss
To strive to fix her beams which are
  More bright and large than his.

Katherine Philips ('Orinda') (1631–64)

Constancy

I cannot change as others do,
    Though you unjustly scorn;
Since that poor swain that sighs for you
    For you alone was born.
No, Phillis, no; your heart to move
    A surer way I'll try;
And, to revenge my slighted love,
    Will still love on and die.

When killed with grief Amyntas lies,
    And you to mind shall call
The sighs that now unpitied rise,
    The tears that vainly fall –
That welcome hour, that ends this smart,
    Will then begin your pain;
For such a faithful tender heart
    Can never break in vain.

John Wilmot, Earl of Rochester (1647–80)

Love

All thoughts, all passions, all delights,
Whatever stirs this mortal frame,
All are but ministers of Love,
    And feed his sacred flame.

Oft in my waking dreams do I
Live o'er again that happy hour,
When midway on the mount I lay,
    Beside the ruined tower.

The moonshine, stealing o'er the scene,
Had blended with the lights of eve;
And she was there, my hope, my joy,
    My own dear Genevieve!

She leaned against the armèd man,
The statue of the armèd Knight;
She stood and listened to my lay,
    Amid the lingering light.

Few sorrows hath she of her own,
My hope! my joy! my Genevieve!
She loves me best whene'er I sing
    The songs that make her grieve.

I played a soft and doleful air;
I sang an old and moving story –
An old rude song, that suited well
    That ruin wild and hoary.

119

She listened with a flitting blush,
With downcast eyes and modest grace;
For well she knew I could not choose
    But gaze upon her face.

I told her of the Knight that wore
Upon his shield a burning brand;
And that for ten long years he wooed
    The Lady of the Land.

I told her how he pined: and ah!
The deep, the low, the pleading tone
With which I sang another's love,
    Interpreted my own.

She listened with a flitting blush,
With downcast eyes, and modest grace;
And she forgave me, that I gazed
    Too fondly on her face!

But when I told the cruel scorn
That crazed that bold and lovely Knight,
And that he crossed the mountain-woods,
    Nor rested day nor night;

That sometimes from the savage den,
And sometimes from the darksome shade,
And sometimes starting up at once
    In green and sunny glade –

There came and looked him in the face
An angel beautiful and bright;
And that he knew it was a Fiend,
    This miserable Knight!

And that, unknowing what he did,
He leaped amid a murderous band,
And saved from outrage worse than death
    The Lady of the Land; –

And how she wept and clasped his knees;
And how she tended him in vain –
And ever strove to expiate
    The scorn that crazed his brain; –

And that she nursed him in a cave;
And how his madness went away,
When on the yellow forest leaves
    A dying man he lay; –

His dying words – but when I reached
That tenderest strain of all the ditty,
My faltering voice and pausing harp
    Disturbed her soul with pity!

All impulses of soul and sense
Had thrilled my guileless Genevieve;
The music and the doleful tale,
    The rich and balmy eve;

And hopes, and fears that kindle hope,
An undistinguishable throng,
And gentle wishes long subdued,
    Subdued and cherished long!

She wept with pity and delight,
She blushed with love and virgin shame;
And like the murmur of a dream,
    I heard her breathe my name.

Her bosom heaved – she stepped aside,
As conscious of my look she stept –
Then suddenly, with timorous eye
    She fled to me and wept.

She half enclosed me with her arms,
She pressed me with a meek embrace;
And bending back her head, looked up,
    And gazed upon my face.

'Twas partly love, and partly fear,
And partly 'twas a bashful art,
That I might rather feel, than see.
    The swelling of her heart.

I calmed her fears, and she was calm,
And told her love with virgin pride;
And so I won my Genevieve,
    My bright and beauteous Bride.

Samuel Taylor Coleridge (1772–1834)

My Delight and Thy Delight

My delight and thy delight
Walking, like two angels white,
In the gardens of the night:

My desire and thy desire
Twining to a tongue of fire,
Leaping live, and laughing higher:

Through the everlasting strife
In the mystery of life.

Love, from whom the world begun,
Hath the secret of the sun.

Love can tell, and love alone,
Whence the million stars were strewn,
Why each atom knows its own,
How, in spite of woe and death,
Gay is life, and sweet is breath:

This he taught us, this we knew,
Happy in his science true,
Hand in hand as we stood
'Neath the shadows of the wood,
Heart to heart as we lay
In the dawning of the day.

Robert Bridges (1844–1930)

Aubade

(*An open Gallery to* JULIET's *Chamber, overlooking the Garden*)

[*Enter* ROMEO *and* JULIET]

JULIET

Wilt thou be gone? It is not yet near day:
It was the nightingale, and not the lark,
That pierced the fearful hollow of thine ear;
Nightly she sings on yond pomegranate tree:
Believe me, love, it was the nightingale.

ROMEO

It was the lark, the herald of the morn,
No nightingale. Look, love, what envious streaks
Do lace the severing clouds in yonder east:
Night's candles are burnt out, and jocund day
Stands tiptoe on the misty mountain tops.
I must be gone and live, or stay and die.

JULIET

Yond light is not daylight, I know it, I:
It is some meteor that the sun exhales
To be to thee this night a torch-bearer
And light thee on the way to Mantua:
Therefore stay yet, thou need'st not to be gone.

ROMEO

Let me be ta'en, let me be put to death;
I am content, so thou wilt have it so.
I'll say yon grey is not the morning's eye,
'Tis but the pale reflex of Cynthia's brow;

Nor that is not the lark whose notes do beat
The vaulty heaven so high above our heads:
I have more care to stay than will to go. –
Come, death, and welcome! Juliet wills it so. –
How is't, my soul? let's talk, – it is not day.

JULIET

It is, it is! – hie hence, be gone, away!
It is the lark that sings so out of tune,
Straining harsh discords and unpleasing sharps.
Some say the lark makes sweet division;
This doth not so, for she divideth us:
Some say the lark and loathed toad changed eyes;
O, now I would they had changed voices too!
Since arm from arm that voice doth us affray,
Hunting thee hence with hunt's-up to the day.
O, now be gone; more light and light it grows.

ROMEO

More light and light, – more dark and dark our woes!

Romeo and Juliet, Act 3 Scene 5
William Shakespeare (1564–1616)

The Sun Rising

Busy old fool, unruly sun,
        Why dost thou thus
Through windows and through curtains call on us?
Must to thy motions lovers' seasons run?
        Saucy pedantic wretch, go chide
        Late schoolboys and sour prentices,
    Go tell court huntsmen that the King will ride,
    Call country ants to harvest offices;
Love, all alike, no season knows nor clime,
Nor hours, days, months, which are the rags of time.

        Thy Beams, so reverend and strong
        Why shouldst thou think?
I could eclipse and cloud them with a wink,
But that I would not lose her sight so long;
        If her eyes have not blinded thine,
        Look, and tomorrow late, tell me,
    Whether both th' Indias of spice and mine
    Be where thou leftst them, or lie here with me.
Ask for those kings whom thou saw'st yesterday,
And thou shalt hear, All here in one bed lay.

        She is all states, and all princes I,
        Nothing else is.
Princes do but play us; compared to this,
All honour's mimic, all wealth alchemy.
        Thou, sun, art half as happy as we,
        In that the world's contracted thus;

Thine age asks ease, and since thy duties be
To warm the world, that's done in warming us.
Shine here to us, and thou art everywhere;
This bed thy centre is, these walls thy sphere.

John Donne (1572–1631)

The Ecstasy

Where, like a pillow on a bed,
    A pregnant bank swelled up, to rest
The violet's reclining head,
    Sat we two, one another's best.

Our hands were firmly cemented
    With a fast balm which thence did spring;
Our eye-beams twisted, and did thread
    Our eyes upon one double string;

So to intergraft our hands, as yet
    Was all the means to make us one,
And pictures in our eyes to get
    Was all our propagation.

As 'twixt two equal armies Fate
    Suspends uncertain victory,
Our souls (which to advance their state
    Were gone out) hung 'twixt her and me.

And whilst our souls negotiate there,
    We like sepulchral statues lay;
All day, the same our postures were,
    And we said nothing, all the day.

If any, so by love refined
    That he soul's language understood,
And by good love were grown all mind,
    Within convenient distance stood,

He (though he knew not which soul spake,
    Because both meant, both spake the same)
Might thence a new concoction take
    And part far purer than he came.

This ecstasy doth unperplex,
    (We said) and tell us what we love;
We see by this it was not sex,
    We see we saw not what did move;

But as all several souls contain
    Mixture of things, they know not what,
Love these mixed souls doth mix again
    And makes both one, each this and that.

A single violet transplant,
    The strength, the colour, and the size
(All which before was poor and scant)
    Redoubles still, and multiplies.

When love with one another so
    Interinanimates two souls,
That abler soul, which thence doth flow,
    Defects of loneliness controls.

We then, who are this new soul, know
    Of what we are composed and made,
For th' atomies of which we grow
    Are souls, whom no change can invade.

But O alas, so long, so far
    Our bodies why do we forbear?

They are ours, though they are not we; we are
    The intelligences, they the sphere.

We owe them thanks, because they thus
    Did us to us at first convey,
Yielded their forces, sense, to us,
    Nor are dross to us, but allay.

On man heaven's influence works not so
    But that it first imprints the air:
So soul into the soul may flow,
    Though it to body first repair.

As our blood labours to beget
    Spirits as like souls as it can,
Because such fingers need to knit
    That subtle knot which makes us man,

So must pure lovers' souls descend
    T' affections, and to faculties
Which sense may reach and apprehend;
    Else a great prince in prison lies.

To our bodies turn we then, that so
    Weak men on love revealed may look;
Love's mysteries in souls do grow,
    But yet the body is his book.

And if some lover, such as we,
    Have heard this dialogue of one,
Let him still mark us; he shall see
    Small change when we are to bodies gone.

John Donne (1572–1631)

Doing, a Filthy Pleasure is, and Short

Doing, a filthy pleasure is, and short;
And done, we straight repent us of the sport:
Let us not then rush blindly on unto it,
Like lustful beasts, that only know to do it:
For lust will languish, and that heat decay
But thus, thus, keeping endless Holy-day
Let us together closely lie, and kiss,
There is no labour, nor no shame in this;
This hath pleased, doth please, and long will please; never
Can this decay, but is beginning ever.

Petronius Arbiter (*c.* 27–66 AD)
Translated by Ben Jonson (1572/3–1637)

Love is
a Sickness

Love is a Sickness

Love is a sickness full of woes,
   All remedies refusing;
A plant that with most cutting grows,
   Most barren with best using.
             Why so?
More we enjoy it, more it dies;
If not enjoyed, it sighing cries –
             Heigh ho!

Love is a torment of the mind,
   A tempest everlasting;
And Jove hath made it of a kind
   Not well, nor full nor fasting.
             Why so?
More we enjoy it, more it dies;
If not enjoyed, it sighing cries –
             Heigh ho!

Samuel Daniel (1562–1619)

Love in Fantastic Triumph Sate

Love in fantastic triumph sate
    Whilst bleeding hearts around him flowed,
For whom fresh pains he did create
    And strange tyrannic power he showed:
From thy bright eyes he took his fires,
    Which round about in sport he hurled;
But 'twas from mine he took desires
    Enough t' undo the amorous world.

From me he took his sighs and tears,
    From thee his pride and cruelty;
From me his languishments and fears,
    And every killing dart from thee.
Thus thou and I the god have armed
    And set him up a deity;
But my poor heart alone is harmed,
    Whilst thine the victor is, and free!

Aphra Behn (1640–89)

Ye Banks and Braes o' Bonnie Doon

Ye banks and braes o' bonnie Doon,
    How can ye bloom sae fair?
How can ye chant, ye little birds,
    And I sae fu' o' care?

Thou'll break my heart, thou bonnie bird
    That sings upon the bough;
Thou minds me o' the happy days
    When my fause Luve was true.

Thou'll break my heart, thou bonnie bird
    That sings beside thy mate;
For sae I sat, and sae I sang,
    And wist na o' my fate.

Aft hae I roved by bonnie Doon
    To see the woodbine twine:
And ilka bird sang o' its Luve,
    And sae did I o' mine.

Wi' lightsome heart I pulled a rose,
    Frae aff its thorny tree;
And my fause Luver staw the rose
    But left the thorn wi' me.

Robert Burns (1759–96)

La Belle Dame Sans Merci

'O what can ail thee, knight-at-arms,
　　Alone and palely loitering?
The sedge has wither'd from the lake,
　　　　And no birds sing.

'O what can ail thee, knight-at-arms!
　　So haggard and so woe-begone?
The squirrel's granary is full,
　　　　And the harvest's done.

'I see a lily on thy brow
　　With anguish moist and fever-dew.
And on thy cheeks a fading rose
　　　　Fast withereth too.'

'I met a lady in the meads,
　　Full beautiful – a faery's child,
Her hair was long, her foot was light,
　　　　And her eyes were wild.

'I made a garland for her head,
　　And bracelets too, and fragrant zone;
She look'd at me as she did love,
　　　　And made sweet moan.

'I set her on my pacing steed,
　　And nothing else saw all day long;
For sidelong would she bend, and sing
　　　　A faery's song.

'She found me roots of relish sweet,
  And honey wild and manna-dew;
And sure in language strange she said,
    "I love thee true."

'She took me to her elfin grot,
  And there she wept and sigh'd full sore;
And there I shut her wild, wild eyes
    With kisses four.

'And there she lullèd me asleep,
  And there I dream'd—ah! woe betide!
The latest dream I ever dream'd
    On the cold hill's side.

'I saw pale kings and princes too,
  Pale warriors, death-pale were they all:
They cried, "La belle Dame sans Merci
    Hath thee in thrall!"

'I saw their starved lips in the gloam
  With horrid warning gapèd wide,
And I awoke and found me here
    On the cold hill's side.

'And this is why I sojourn here
  Alone and palely loitering,
Though the sedge is wither'd from the lake,
    And no birds sing.'

John Keats (1795–1821)

I Cannot Live Without My Life

The master looked asleep, and I ventured soon after sunrise to quit the room and steal out to the pure refreshing air. The servants thought me gone to shake off the drowsiness of my protracted watch; in reality, my chief motive was seeing Mr Heathcliff. If he had remained among the larches all night, he would have heard nothing of the stir at the Grange; unless, perhaps, he might catch the gallop of the messenger going to Gimmerton. If he had come nearer, he would probably be aware, from the lights flitting to and fro, and the opening and shutting of the outer doors, that all was not right within. I wished, yet feared, to find him. I felt the terrible news must be told, and I longed to get it over; but how to do it I did not know. He was there – at least, a few yards further in the park; leant against an old ash-tree, his hat off, and his hair soaked with the dew that had gathered on the budded branches, and fell pattering round him. He had been standing a long time in that position, for I saw a pair of ousels passing and repassing scarcely three feet from him, busy in building their nest, and regarding his proximity no more than that of a piece of timber. They flew off at my approach, and he raised his eyes and spoke: – 'She's dead!' he said; 'I've not waited for you to learn that. Put your handkerchief away – don't snivel before me. Damn you all! she wants none of your tears!'

I was weeping as much for him as her: we do sometimes pity creatures that have none of the feeling either for themselves or others. When I first looked into his face, I perceived that he had got intelligence of the catastrophe;

and a foolish notion struck me that his heart was quelled and he prayed, because his lips moved and his gaze was bent on the ground.

'Yes, she's dead!' I answered, checking my sobs and drying my cheeks. 'Gone to heaven, I hope; where we may, every one, join her, if we take due warning and leave our evil ways to follow good!'

'Did she take due warning, then?' asked Heathcliff, attempting a sneer. 'Did she die like a saint? Come, give me a true history of the event. How did – ?'

He endeavoured to pronounce the name, but could not manage it; and compressing his mouth he held a silent combat with his inward agony, defying, meanwhile, my sympathy with an unflinching, ferocious stare. 'How did she die?' he resumed, at last – fain, notwithstanding his hardihood, to have a support behind him; for, after the struggle, he trembled, in spite of himself, to his very finger-ends.

'Poor wretch!' I thought; 'you have a heart and nerves the same as your brother men! Why should you be anxious to conceal them? Your pride cannot blind God! You tempt him to wring them, till he forces a cry of humiliation.'

'Quietly as a lamb!' I answered, aloud. 'She drew a sigh, and stretched herself, like a child reviving, and sinking again to sleep; and five minutes after I felt one little pulse at her heart, and nothing more!'

'And – did she ever mention me?' he asked, hesitating, as if he dreaded the answer to his question would introduce details that he could not bear to hear.

'Her senses never returned: she recognised nobody from the time you left her,' I said. 'She lies with a sweet smile on her face; and her latest ideas wandered back to pleasant early days. Her life closed in a gentle dream – may she wake as kindly in the other world!'

'May she wake in torment!' he cried, with frightful vehemence, stamping his foot, and groaning in a sudden paroxysm of ungovernable passion. 'Why, she's a liar to the end! Where is she? Not there – not in heaven – not perished – where? Oh! you said you cared nothing for my sufferings! And I pray one prayer – I repeat it till my tongue stiffens – Catherine Earnshaw, may you not rest as long as I am living; you said I killed you – haunt me, then! The murdered do haunt their murderers, I believe. I know that ghosts have wandered on earth. Be with me always – take any form – drive me mad! only do not leave me in this abyss, where I cannot find you! Oh, God! it is unutterable! I cannot live without my life! I can not live without my soul!'

Wuthering Heights
Emily Brontë (1818–48)

Lord Ullin's Daughter

A Chieftain to the Highlands bound
  Cries 'Boatman, do not tarry!
And I'll give thee a silver pound
  To row us o'er the ferry!'

– 'Now, who be ye, would cross Lochgyle
  This dark and stormy water?'
– 'O I'm the chief of Ulva's isle,
  And this, Lord Ullin's daughter.'

'And fast before her father's men
  Three days we've fled together,
For should he find us in the glen,
  My blood would stain the heather.'

'His horsemen hard behind us ride –
  Should they our steps discover,
Then who will cheer my bonny bride
  When they have slain her lover?'

Out spoke the hardy Highland wight,
  'I'll go, my chief, I'm ready;
It is not for your silver bright,
  But for your winsome lady: –'

'And by my word! The bonny bird
  In danger shall not tarry;
So though the waves are raging white,
  I'll row you o'er the ferry.'

By this the storm grew loud apace,
    The water-wraith was shrieking;
And in the scowl of heaven each face
    Grew dark as they were speaking.

But still as wilder blew the wind,
    And as the night grew drearer,
Adown the glen rode armed men,
    Their trampling sounded nearer.

'Oh haste thee, haste!' the lady cries,
    'Though tempests round us gather;
I'll meet the raging of the skies,
    But not an angry father!'

The boat has left a stormy land,
    A stormy sea before her, –
When, O! too strong for human hand
    The tempest gathered o'er her.

And still they rowed amidst the roar
    Of waters fast prevailing:
Lord Ullin reached that fatal shore, –
    His wrath was changed to wailing.

For, sore dismayed, through storm and shade
    His child he did discover: –
One lovely hand she stretched for aid,
    And one was round her lover.

'Come back! Come back!' he cried in grief
    Across this stormy water:
And I'll forgive your Highland chief: –
    My daughter! O my daughter!'

'Twas vain: the loud waves lashed the shore,
    Return or aid preventing:
The waters wild went o'er his child,
    And he was left lamenting.

Thomas Campbell (1777–1844)

I Need Not Go

I need not go
Through sleet and snow
To where I know
She waits for me;
She will tarry me there
Till I find it fair,
And have time to spare
From company.

When I've overgot
The world somewhat,
When things cost not
Such stress and strain,
Is soon enough
By cypress sough
To tell my Love
I am come again.

And if some day,
When none cries nay,
I still delay
To seek her side,
(Though ample measure
Of fitting leisure
Await my pleasure)
She will riot chide.

What – not upbraid me
That I delayed me,
Nor ask what stayed me
So long? Ah, no! –
New cares may claim me,
New loves inflame me,
She will not blame me,
But suffer it so.

Thomas Hardy (1840–1928)

A Rondel of Love

Lo, what it is to love
Learn ye that list to prove,
By me, I say, that no ways may
The ground of grief remove,
But still decay both nicht and day:
Lo, what it is to love!

Love is ane fervent fire
Kindlit without desire,
Short pleasure, long displeasure,
Repentance is the hire;
Ane pure tressour without measour;
Love is ane fervent fire.

To love and to be wise,
To rage with good advice;
Now thus, now than, so gois the game,
Incertain is the dice;
There is no man, I say, that can
Both love and to be wise.

Flee always from the snare,
Learn at me to beware;
It is ane pain, and double trane
Of endless woe and care;
For to refrain that danger plain,
Flee always from the snare.

Alexander Scott (16th century)

The Appeal: An Earnest Suit to His Unkind Mistress, Not to Forsake Him

And wilt thou leave me thus!
Say nay, say nay, for shame!
– To save thee from the blame
Of all my grief and grame.
And wilt thou leave me thus?
　Say nay! say nay!

And wilt thou leave me thus,
That hath loved thee so long
In wealth and woe among:
And is thy heart so strong
As for to leave me thus?
　Say nay! say nay!

And wilt thou leave me thus,
That hath given thee my heart
Never for to depart
Neither for pain nor smart:
And wilt thou leave me thus?
　Say nay! say nay!

And wilt thou leave me thus,
And have no more pity
Of him that loveth thee?
Alas, thy cruelty!
And wilt thou leave me thus?
　Say nay! say nay!

Sir Thomas Wyatt (1503–42)

Prayer for Indifference

I ask no kind return of love,
　　No tempting charm to please;
Far from the heart those gifts remove,
　　That sighs for peace and ease.

Nor peace nor ease the heart can know,
　　That, like the needle true,
Turns at the touch of joy or woe,
　　But turning, trembles too.

Far as distress the soul can wound,
　　'Tis pain in each degree:
'Tis bliss but to a certain bound,
　　Beyond is agony.

Fanny Greville (18th century)

An Evening at Uppercross

The evening ended with dancing. On its being proposed, Anne offered her services, as usual; and though her eyes would sometimes fill with tears as she sat at the instrument, she was extremely glad to be employed, and desired nothing in return but to be unobserved.

It was a merry, joyous party, and no one seemed in higher spirits than Captain Wentworth. She felt that he had every thing to elevate him which general attention and deference, and especially the attention of all the young women, could do. The Miss Hayters, the females of the family of cousins already mentioned, were apparently admitted to the honour of being in love with him; and as for Henrietta and Louisa, they both seemed so entirely occupied by him, that nothing but the continued appearance of the most perfect good-will between themselves could have made it credible that they were not decided rivals. If he were a little spoilt by such universal, such eager admiration, who could wonder?

These were some of the thoughts which occupied Anne, while her fingers were mechanically at work, proceeding for half an hour together, equally without error, and without consciousness. Once she felt that he was looking at herself, observing her altered features, perhaps, trying to trace in them the ruins of the face which had once charmed him; and once she knew that he must have spoken of her; she was hardly aware of it, till she heard the answer; but then she was sure of his having asked his partner whether Miss Elliot never danced? The answer was, 'Oh, no; never; she has quite given up dancing. She had rather play. She is never tired of playing.' Once, too, he spoke to her. She had left the instrument on the dancing being over, and he had sat down to try to make out an air which he wished to give the Miss Musgroves an idea of. Unintentionally she returned to that part of the room; he saw her, and, instantly rising, said, with studied politeness –

'I beg your pardon, madam, this is your seat;' and though she immediately drew back with a decided negative, he was not to be induced to sit down again.

Anne did not wish for more of such looks and speeches. His cold politeness, his ceremonious grace, were worse than anything.

Persuasion
Jane Austen (1775–1817)

Balthasar's Song

Sigh no more, ladies, sigh no more;
    Men were deceivers ever;
One foot in sea and one on shore,
    To one thing constant never;
Then sigh not so, But let them go,
    And be you blithe and bonny;
Converting all your sounds of woe
    Into hey nonny, nonny.

Sing no more ditties, sing no more,
    Of dumps so dull and heavy;
The fraud of men was ever so,
    Since summer first was leafy.
Then sigh not so, But let them go,
    And be you blithe and bonny,
Converting all your sounds of woe
    Into hey, nonny, nonny.

Much Ado About Nothing, Act 2 Scene 3
William Shakespeare (1564–1616)

Rivals

Of all the torments, all the cares,
    With which our lives are cursed
Of all the plagues a lover bears,
    Sure rivals are the worst!
By partners in each other kind
    Afflictions easier grow;
In love alone we hate to find
    Companions of our woe.

Sylvia, for all the pangs you see
    Are labouring in my breast,
I beg not you would favour me,
    Would you but slight the rest!
How great soe'er your rigours are,
    With them alone I'll cope;
I can endure my own despair,
    But not another's hope.

William Walsh (1663–1708)

To Lucasta, Going to the Wars

Tell me not, Sweet, I am unkind,
    That from the nunnery
Of thy chaste breast and quiet mind
    To war and arms I fly.

True, a new mistress now I chase,
    The first foe in the field;
And with a stronger faith embrace
    A sword, a horse, a shield.

Yet this inconstancy is such
    As thou too shalt adore;
I could not love thee, Dear, so much,
    Loved I not Honour more.

Richard Lovelace (1618–57/8)

Female Inconstancy

My mistress says she'll marry none but me;
No, not if Jove himself a suitor be.
She says so; but what women say to kind
Lovers, we write in rapid streams and wind.

Catullus (87–57 BC)
Translated by Richard Lovelace (1618–57/8)

The Lover's Resolution

Shall I, wasting in despair,
Die because a woman's fair?
Or make pale my cheeks with care
'Cause another's rosy are?
Be she fairer than the day,
Or the flow'ry meads in May,
   If she think not well of me,
   What care I how fair she be?

Shall my silly heart be pined
'Cause I see a woman kind?
Or a well disposèd nature
Joinèd with a lovely feature?
Be she meeker, kinder, than
Turtle-dove or pelican,
   If she be not so to me,
   What care I how kind she be?

Shall a woman's virtues move
Me to perish for her love?
Or her well-deservings known
Make me quite forget my own?
Be she with that goodness blest
Which may merit name of best,
   If she be not such to me,
   What care I how good she be?

'Cause her fortune seems too high,
Shall I play the fool and die?
She that bears a noble mind,
If not outward helps she find,
Thinks what with them he would do
That without them dares her woo;
   And unless that mind I see,
   What care I how great she be?

Great, or good, or kind, or fair,
I will ne'er the more despair;
If she love me, this believe,
I will die ere she shall grieve;
If she slight me when I woo,
I can scorn and let her go;
   For if she be not for me,
   What care I for whom she be?

George Wither (1588–1667)

Since There's No Help,
Come Let Us Kiss and Part

Since there's no help, come let us kiss and part,
Nay, I have done: you get no more of me,
And I am glad, yea glad with all my heart,
That thus so cleanly I myself can free.
Shake hands for ever, cancel all our vows,
And when we meet at any time again
Be it not seen in either of our brows
That we one jot of former love retain.
Now at the last gasp of Love's latest breath,
When his pulse failing, Passion speechless lies,
When Faith is kneeling by his bed of death,
And Innocence is closing up his eyes,
    Now, if thou wouldst, when all have given him over,
    From death to life thou might'st him yet recover.

Michael Drayton (1563–1631)

The Prisoner

He did not wear his scarlet coat,
    For blood and wine are red,
And blood and wine were on his hands
    When they found him with the dead,
The poor dead woman whom he loved,
    And murdered in her bed.

He walked amongst the Trial Men
    In a suit of shabby gray;
A cricket cap was on his head,
    And his step seemed light and gay;
But I never saw a man who looked
    So wistfully at the day.

I never saw a man who looked
    With such a wistful eye
Upon that little tent of blue
    Which prisoners call the sky,
And at every drifting cloud that went
    With sails of silver by.

I walked, with other souls in pain,
    Within another ring,
And was wondering if the man had done
    A great or little thing,
When a voice behind me whispered low,
    'That fellow's got to swing.'

Dear Christ! the very prison walls
    Suddenly seemed to reel,
And the sky above my head became
    Like a casque of scorching steel;
And, though I was a soul in pain,
    My pain I could not feel.

I only knew what haunted thought
    Quickened his step, and why
He looked upon the garish day
    With such a wistful eye;
The man had killed the thing he loved,
    And so he had to die.

Yet each man kills the thing he loves,
    By each let this be heard,
Some do it with a bitter look,
    Some with a flattering word,
The coward does it with a kiss,
    The brave man with a sword!

Some kill their love when they are young,
    And some when they are old;
Some strangle with the hands of Lust,
    Some with the hands of Gold:
The kindest use a knife, because
    The dead so soon grow cold.

Some love too little, some too long,
    Some sell, and others buy;

Some do the deed with many tears,
    And some without a sigh:
For each man kills the thing he loves,
    Yet each man does not die.

He does not die a death of shame
    On a day of dark disgrace,
Nor have a noose about his neck,
    Nor a cloth upon his face,
Nor drop feet foremost through the floor
  Into an empty space.

He does not sit with silent men
    Who watch him night and day;
Who watch him when he tries to weep,
    And when he tries to pray;
Who watch him lest himself should rob
    The prison of its prey.

He does not wake at dawn to see
    Dread figures throng his room,
The shivering Chaplain robed in white,
    The Sheriff stern with gloom,
And the Governor all in shiny black,
    With the yellow face of Doom.

He does not rise in piteous haste
    To put on convict-clothes,
While some coarse-mouthed Doctor gloats, and notes
    Each new and nerve-twitched pose,

Fingering a watch whose little ticks
    Are like horrible hammer-blows.

He does not feel that sickening thirst
    That sands one's throat, before
The hangman with his gardener's gloves
    Comes through the padded door,
And binds one with three leathern thongs,
    That the throat may thirst no more.

He does not bend his head to hear
    The Burial Office read,
Nor, while the anguish of his soul
    Tells him he is not dead,
Cross his own coffin, as he moves
    Into the hideous shed.

He does not stare upon the air
    Through a little roof of glass:
He does not pray with lips of clay
    For his agony to pass;
Nor feel upon his shuddering cheek
    The kiss of Caiaphas.

The Ballad of Reading Gaol
Oscar Wilde (1854–1900)

The Apparition

When by thy scorn, O murd'ress, I am dead,
And that thou thinkst thee free
From all solicitation from me,
Then shall my ghost come to thy bed,
And thee, feigned vestal, in worse arms shall see:
Then thy sick taper will begin to wink,
And he, whose thou art then, being tired before,
Will, if thou stir, or pinch to wake him, think
      Thou call'st for more,
And, in false sleep, will from thee shrink:
And then, poor aspen wretch, neglected thou
Bathed in a cold quicksilver sweat wilt lie,
      A verier ghost than I.
What I will say, I will not tell thee now,
Lest that preserve thee; and since my love is spent,
I'd rather thou shouldst painfully repent,
Than by my threatenings rest still innocent.

John Donne (1572–1631)

Index of First Lines

Index of Authors